SELF

AUTHOR: ONYEKACHI KENIS

*Life is beautiful because of your essence that permeates the space
in which you fill.*

TABLE OF CONTENT

FOREWORD

If you want me to be honest, it's really hard to finish something while experiencing the struggles of life at the same time. Although there are good things that I have experienced, I for some reason feel like the bad sticks to the skin more. Now I know that I am not perfect and I know that I am bound to make tons of mistakes, but it doesn't mean that I should be treated less than what I am. It's so cliche to say that everyone makes mistakes, but it's so true. We live in a world where those who hide the flaws the best get praised, and those who show it for the world to see get frowned upon. We all have flaws, never forget that.

FOREWORD

I do want to say that I am truly grateful to have finished this book. It goes over finite details on different qualities and ways one can discover self. I realized that I have been through enough shit, and survived it to be able to help guide those to a discovery of the self, and how to overcome challenges that we put onto ourselves. I was never the kid that really got heard anywhere, so I am hoping that the words that I have written can enlighten you and change your perspective about yourself and the world. I am not God, nor am I an angel sent from heaven, I am just a young man, who got the luxury to fail earlier in life, who got a chance to experience both sides of the spectrum in life.

I've experienced both good, and evil, success and failure, rich at heart, and broken in spirit. I feel like I have experienced so much mental exhaustion and physical wear and tear, most having to do with a broken family, unstable home, poverty, neglect, hardship and a whole lot of other gruesome experiences. I think I began to develop joy by being able to witness my transformation of rising above all of that, and really being able to embody a glowing

<u>FOREWORD</u>

spirit. It's fascinating when one begins to discover life by simple observation, you may really be looking at the answers the whole time without even noticing. I started to understand that this world that I live in belongs to me, same as for you. Therefore you live this life as if it belongs to you, avoid the eyes of others that seem to tear you down, and move towards those eyes that makes you feel good. Why live a life of misery when you have the ability to choose?

CHAPTER ONE
SELF

I am not inferior or superior to no one,
I am just myself.
                              -Onyekachi Kenis

I was literally on the border line of insanity

when it came down to me figuring out my next big

move in life. It was like one day I would be so

amped up to the point where I'd actually feel the

adrenaline rushing through my veins, and then the

next day or so, I would be back to dragging my feet

through the floor with a hunched back wondering,

where the hell did all my confidence go? I would catch myself trying to escape this mental prison that I was creating for myself. It felt like finally getting your hands on the key to unlock that door of the small room you were in; only to find out that you were trapped inside an entirely different room this whole time.

I was the type of person that would wait for the outside world to change before I would change. When times got rough, I would blame any and everybody for their lack of effort in understanding why my life was so miserable. I'd get mad at everything, like a crazy driver almost ramming my car on the highway or an innocent bystander just having a problem with staring, I would even get mad at the sun for being so freakin' hot during the damn summer! Honestly, I thought everyone and everything was out to get me, I didn't know what to do but to react in anger and frustration. This sometimes led to a downward spiral of regret and resentment. I'd always felt like the type of person that was never good enough, I felt like I wasn't deserving of the things that I wanted in my life or worked hard for. I would wallow in self pity when I felt like I wasn't doing better than my peers, I would even engage in destructive habits just to escape this self-inflicted misery that I created at the moment. This would go on for days, weeks and even months. Then, I would suddenly snap back into reality and boy oh boy, here comes the thrill of the adrenaline rush again. Afterwards, I would have this feeling that I could take on the world and that nothing can stop me. Then, I would find myself back in this ridiculous cycle of self torture. Now, "self torture" may be a bit of an overstatement, but technically if I were include the fact that I was literally creating the sequence of my own agitated events as well as giving way to consistent irresponsible behaviors, only to be annoyed at my results which forced me to ameliorate, then "self torture" is the perfect term to use my friend.

I realized that we as human beings come from all walks of life and we've been given something called "THE GREAT FREE WILL", which basically means that we can do anything that we want, I mean ANYTHING! One of my greatest discoveries I've been able to come across is that we are not our bodies, we simply reside in our bodies. I believe this is what allowed me to register the fact that "THE GREAT FREE WILL" is so powerful.

I feel like I have one of the weirdest perceptions of human beings today. Honestly, I feel like we all live in this super high tech gadget sort of like a robot so to say, which is known as the human body, and this "robot" has the ability to connect with its natural habitat as well as with different "robots" of its kind . This robot, I believe, possesses the essence of who we really are and it is our job as the essence of creation to learn how to utilize this body to the best of its ability. Don't ask me how I came up with this perception, I think it makes a whole lot of sense and plus it's a pretty cool concept. This on the other leads me back to why I believe THE GREAT FREE WILL is so freaking awesome. Most of us have been placed in this high performance machine (the body) and don't even know how to properly use it. THE GREAT FREE WILL might have been an effective factor for us when we were much younger due to our keen sense of imagination, but it's like our authority figures were always there to ruin the fun, am I right? As we grow older, we start to make sense of this GREAT FREE WILL. For some, they begin to use it in accomplishing big goals and tasks that they set out for themselves while for others, they use this freedom to explore irrelevant miscellaneous features that this "robot" comes with.

While making use of this great power I have been able to discover parts of myself that I just never knew existed and I believe it must've been the things that I was able to experience in my life which lead me to my partial discovery. I say "partial", because we as human beings are filled with endless possibilities, you can never reach a point of complete discovery. There is always room for discovering who it is that you are or who it is you think you can be. I have come to understand that who we truly think that we are, is that power that lies within this fancy high tech gadget which is known as the body. Some of us are able to harness this power in accomplishing big goals, while others find it entirely too difficult to even harness such ability. I was one of the individuals who struggled in developing such power. A wise person who goes by the name of "The mysterious Sol", once told me that "we as human beings allow the lives of others to be projected unto us, therefore allowing us to live as others would live whether good or bad". In layman's terms, 'we conform'. **THE GREAT FREE WILL** gives us the ability to act like anything or anyone. Such individuals we tend to portray are those who "vibe'' the way we think. If one were to possess a quality that we so deeply admire or that we feel resonates with us, more than likely we tend to make it our own, by either subconsciously picking up these traits or by simply intentionally connecting with these individuals whether as a friend, associate or even a business partner. This can sometimes cause one to begin to neglect themselves.

I remember being a young bull trying to figure out this way of life. I could remember how I used to seek validation from others to affirm whether I was being myself the right way, and I began to comprehend that this was a toxic trait that was slowly becoming the way of life for me. Sometimes it was because I would doubt the qualities that I really felt were authentic to me. I remember allowing myself to let others be the judge of the fascinating qualities that I knew I possessed and I realized that if their expectations didn't meet up to how I truly felt about myself, I would begin to indulge into the habit of self disapproval, which would most of the times be the cause of my downward spirals. I would begin to seek for people who accepted me for my flaws and 9 times out of 10 the people that I was seeking, were doing the same thing. These people eventually became my close friends. Some of these friendships led to comfort which became very detrimental to my way of thinking. It would have probably been better if we were doing something much more productive with our time but the truth was we were all too scared to really tap into our evolved self, not everyone wanted to admit that, but that's really what it was.

In order for me to truly understand this observation I had to become aware of who I was at the time, I wanted to know what the "TRUE SELF" was .

The TRUE SELF to my understanding is this miraculous entity that lives in the product which we utilize today when making our debut on this Earth. Some like to call this the essences of life, others like to call this the soul, whatever it is, I know that it is amazing, abundant and forever powerful. Our soul, which is who we truly are, has a tendency of being consumed by the things that have been absorbed by this product known as "the human body". Although the product a.k.a human body is a powerful manifestation on its own, we still need to learn how to utilize our soul, which is who we truly are, to tap into these positive traits that this body possesses as well as the negative traits, and to just learn to simply embrace it. One thing that I can say I struggled with was allowing the love that I possessed to pass through me and magnify outward to affect the people I came in contact with. Instead I had a tendency of directing my personal love that was meant for me, to any and everyone that I came across. Which allowed me to feel weak and desperate for attention if the love I gave wasn't reciprocated. This reminds me of the scene in Hercules when Hercules lost his godlike powers because he fell madly in love with the lovely Megara who was really working for Hades the whole time. I'm sure you guys remember Hercules, the famous 1997 Disney movie. Well at least I hope, I wasn't even born around that time but I still watched it so if you haven't got a chance to see it, tell walt disney I sent ya. Anyway, to avoid my digression I made a whole chapter that goes over more about self love. I felt the need to bring this to the light to show the effect that love can have to self and how it tends to destroy "self" when used inappropriately.

Self. This is a term that has raised up a lot of conflict and controversial discussions between the philosophers of our preceding era. David Humes, a renowned Scottish philosopher, defines his concept of self as a connection of multiple impressions into a chain that defines who we are. He believes the idea of having a mind, body, and soul is an illusion, and the act of us talking about such ideas is a natural thing because we exist. Humes believes that we are who we are based on the connected impressions that we tend to make, for example if you give off an impression of someone who is sad all the time, then more than likely individuals would perceive you as a person who has a lot going on in their personal life. This can be said about someone who impresses happiness. This person would then be considered a person who has a lot of good going in their life. I never really knew who David Humes was prior to me making a decision to write this book, but his philosophy on the human self kinda opened a newer level of consciousness for me when it boiled down to trying to figure out who the hell we are. Reason being is because he believed in human feelings, he understood that the feelings of human beings are important when it comes down to teaching a large crowd or even grabbing an audience's attention. He's right. Our feeling plays an important key note when trying to understand self, it enhances our ability to act and sometimes make intelligent decisions. Although this was a popular philosophy back then, I feel like it raises a lot of concerns to the minority. For example, since the slave masters "FELT" like having slaves and flogging them till their backs would shed, does that make it ok?(this is not a slave book) Or, "tech giants" who "FEEL" like taking advantage of the minds of the uninitiated to avoid an over turn of power in the territorial domain, does that also make it ok? Our feelings only work to an extent when backed by something. There always has to be a limit somewhere otherwise it'll just be too much. The moment David Humes said he doesn't believe that these bodies do not maintain a soul was where

I had to draw the line. Now I don't want to make this book about what past philosophers or historians believe themselves to be, but I do have to provide some type of factual evidence to support my claims.

Like I said before we are the power that lies within this product called the body, the sooner we are able to distinguish between the two the faster our lives become easier. There are three components that make up who it is that we are, and that is the Mind, the Body, and the Soul. I have spent the last two and a half years seeking information from humanity gurus and tech and science geniuses like Dr. Joe Dispenza, The Great Bob Proctor, Sadghuru and many more. Now I have made it my job to help you understand what I was able to learn from these unique individuals, my perception of these three components (mind, body, soul), and how they correlate with one another like a gear machine. First things first the mind.

~*THE MIND*~

The mind is where all things are created both good and bad. This is said to be the road map to our truest most authenticated self. I explained a little bit about the mind in my first book "You Already Possess It" and I explained how the mind can be divided into two parts: the conscious and the subconscious mind. In this book I will try my best to dive a little deeper and give you guys a more crystalized understanding of these two minds and how it can influence the "TRUE SELF".

It has been said that the conscious mind is the fundamental core when defining human nature. The conscious mind is the originator of thought and it is responsible for important day to day decision making. The conscious mind controls what we presently hear, see, smell, taste, and touch. In other words it controls our 5 major senses. So anytime you smell a batch of warm chocolate chip cookies, or hear a friend calling out your name to get your attention, just remember that it is your conscious mind actively at work.

The conscious mind is a key component when understanding oneself because it helps deal with defining a clear mental picture of our ideal self. I realized that anytime I were to wind up in an unfortunate situation, it would always result in a new idea from my conscious thinking that got me out of that situation. The consciousness is the image-making power house of the mind which helps with fantasizing, memory and perception, intuition etc. it is responsible for distinguishing this from that. It helps us with the awareness of qualities which one possesses.

This body is equipped with a lot of fancy features that can help us grow and evolve into a higher self and if you want to know the cool things that this awesome high tech gadget can do, your conscious mind can help you to discover this.

I honestly didn't think writing a book would be such a huge deal until I wrote my first one. I didn't realize that I had the ability to do so. I used to be the kind of guy that would spend most of my time with friends and cracking jokes all day. It wasn't until I finally came up with the idea to sit down and write a book that finally gave me a sense of worth in this life. I must say that I'm glad I did so, for some reason I got so much respect from people, everyone I came across kept thinking I was some genius because I wrote a book. Doing this helped me understand how easy it is for one to thrive in this society. I developed so much love, passion and attention for it to the point where it got me writing another book, the one you're reading right now! I was able to understand that one may never know that they have the ability to sing songs, dance, draw, write, or create new inventions if this amazing part of the mind didn't exist.

The conscious mind is the mother of new creations and ideas. This faculty is what gave me the ability to write this book and is what will give you the ability to start on that new project you've been hesitant about once you finish this book. I believe this is what makes us God's highest form of creation and superior to other animals on earth. Consciousness has the ability to influence the emotions of the body which can cause us to feel happy, mad, sad etc. at the new experiences we tend to encounter. One can get so good with this ability to the point where they can consciously influence other people's emotions. Watching a scary movie can be a prime example. The producers and film directors have advanced ways of influencing human emotions with the use of real life experiences. Some may ask how is that even possible? Well I hope that I can be the first to tell you that consciousness has v.i.p access to influence the brain which creates new patterns of neurons that fire together and wire together to produce new emotions throughout the body.

Our brain as some may know is the gray mass of muscle that sits in between our earlobes. It's crazy how the brain is roughly the size of two clenched fist and has so much power and control over the physical body. The brain is connected to the human nervous system which controls the physical functions and feelings of the body.

We as human life robots can use this conscious mind to accept and reject information from the outside world. Information outside of our natural psyche tends to program the subconscious mind.

At one point in my life I was surrounded by negativity and I didn't know how it was going to affect me or my future, I was surrounded by those that thought less of me and the only thing I could do at that time was to simply reject their beliefs and accept my own. I would literally sit down and talk to my body like a pet, and say "the things that they are saying to you are not true, you are strong, you are powerful, you are a success story", and to tell you the truth that shit actually worked. I had to realize that the things that affected my body also affected me as a soul, so if my body is strong then I am strong, if my body is successful then I am successful so on and so forth. People want to have control over you in some way shape or form and you have the power to prevent this from happening. The last thing you want is for someone who has little to no experience in the things that you want to accomplish trying to shape your destiny and tell you what to do. So next time someone were to tell you a piece of information or belief that does not resonate with you, you simply knock that sucker right out of your magnificent aura.

Now that you guys have a somewhat better understanding of consciousness, it's time to dive into a little more fascinating part of the mind which is the sleeping mind. This can also be known as the subconscious mind. This powerful force can be likened to the point where all miracles transpire. This part of the mind is the most inconceivable thing known to mankind when backed by the aid of consciousness. The things that the subconscious mind can do for the life of ourselves as well as the lives of others is by far beyond belief. On my ongoing journey to discovering SELF, the subconscious has been a unique factor to me so far. Unraveling the mysteries of this force and what it has done since the evolution of humanity is still an ongoing topic in this era we live in today, but I will make it my duty to transfer the things that I've been able to stumble across as it pertains to the subconscious mind and how it has been able to help me discover a side of my self that seemed to be hidden for quite some time into that wee little brain of yours.

(Relax, we more than likely got the same size brain, sheesh).

So, what is the subconscious mind? Well, when we think of the subconscious, we think of every habitual behavior that this robot/body produces. Such habits include the natural phenomenon that we have no control over like the habitual pulsating of the heart, the flowing of blood throughout the body, blinking of eyes, even the "simple" act of perspiration. Anything that is done without will or the use of the conscious mind is more than likely the subconscious mind. So let's take this moment and give thanks to that part of the mind for keeping our heart in rhythm while we're asleep and all that other good stuff that goes on in our bodies that we are unaware of.

The subconsciousness is responsible for the genetic program of a human being. This universe we live in has a specific and modified program, and we as human beings are the manifestation of this program. The deeper mind a.k.a the sleeping mind is forever powerful because it affects all aspects of our lives such as the spiritual, the mental, and the physical program. (A program simply means how something was set up, in human terms how we were brought up or raised). Some of us were brought up in the worst conditions. Financial lack, emotional instability, and mental traumatization are usually the effects caused by the poor environments in which people were raised in, like a person's family household, the neighborhoods, even the schools etc. Family members and friends can play a huge toll in the programming of our habitual behaviors, and the worst part about this is that some of them aren't even doing this on purpose. You have to be aware of the damages that they are doing to you, most of the time these individuals that affect our subconscious program have an altered program themselves due to the way they were brought up. Damn. I'm sure you've heard of that term "generational curse" and that one valiant individual that eventually breaks this curse, now this individual may be you, scratch that, this person`~IS YOU~, whatever you do to break out of this curse just know that it is going to involve taking risk on the ideas and believing in the ideas that are created and originated in side the conscious mind and a developed subconscious program to maintain habitual consistency.

It has been said that the subconscious mind is the producer of the results we get out of life. I guess this is due to the habitual behaviors that make up this part of mind. Take a farmer for instance, a farmer knows that in order to get his desired crops during harvest time, he has to develop a habit of consistent care when tending to these crops. A farmer can not water and fertilize crops once or twice, then forget about it, and expect a boat load of substantial vegetables, that's like deciding to get a tattoo of your name on your shoulder and the tattoo artist only stops at the second letter. The farmer is to water these plants day in and day out, apply various pesticides and rodent killer to protect his crops, he is to apply fertilizer to the soil to ensure rapid growth and a healthy plant until he is able to reap the harvest that he has sown. This concept applies to anything that we do in life or any endeavor we decide to take on. We are to condition our body to adapt to certain habits until they have been able to produce the desired results.

One thing that I like about the subconscious mind is that it is the revealer of one's current situation. As you may know, our subconscious mind is our program, basically the way we were brought up. Our program is in direct relation to our condition, and what exactly is a "condition"? Well, a condition is the circumstances affecting the way in which people live or work. And like I said before, we sometimes allow the consciousness of others or the subconscious program of others to affect the way we live, work and even the way we perceive life. I want you to take this moment to consciously look around you and notice your current conditions. If you are not satisfied with these conditions the only thing to consider is changing your subconscious program . This may include changing the people you surround yourself with, your environment and even your own habits.

I'm currently writing this chapter in my uncle's home which kind of sucks. Don't get me wrong it's a beautiful home and I'm truly grateful to be here rather than being out on the streets somewhere, but there are a lot of not so good memories attached to this house that have been imbedded into my subconscious core which have had a way of affecting the way that I've been living my life. This honestly, is one of the reasons why I am writing this book, so that one with profound expertise can recommend my book to the masses and get me to my desired reality. This is a mere dream that may be a bit over the top, but with Faith it's definitely worth a shot.

I'm currently putting the laws of the mind into practical use by using my conscious mind to originate thoughts and ideas and adding to these pages and also by utilizing my subconscious into developing a studying and writing habit which will overall alter my conditions in a positive way, which will lead to the completion of this book. If you are able to understand what has been said in the preceding lines then there shouldn't even be a reason why I should complete this book, but I will for publishing purposes.

The sleeping mind is considered to be the powerful mind because when backed by the conscious mind, it can give us the life that we truly want. The deeper mind is influenced by the conscious mind which defines and controls our day to day activities. This means when we decide to consciously do an activity repeatedly we begin to alter the functions/program of our body which therefore leads to a change in one's habits which ultimately ends in the change of one's lifestyle which then leads to the desired results. This mind is also responsible for our habitual thinking. A famous neuroscientist known as Dr. Joe Dispenza speaks widely on these two powerful minds, and how they influence our lives, and he mentioned one thing that really stood out to me. He said, and I quote "we as human beings think on average about 70,000 thoughts per day and about 90 percent of those thoughts are from the day before, the same thoughts produce the same choices, the same choices lead to the same behavior, same behavior creates the same experience and the same experiences produce the same emotions". It's literally like a little domino effect.

"I was stuck because I was limited by the thoughts and opinions of myself as well as others around me. This allowed me to repeat the same emotions daily, which was the cause of my poor results" ~Onyekachi.

Some of us are unaware that the repeated thoughts were what was shaping the **TRUE SELF** the whole time, and sometimes these are thoughts we don't really feel aroused or moved by. This is most likely the cause of fear, the inability to consciously think for oneself. This can be crippling to one's discovery of self if not acted upon and expressed in a proper fashion. Metacognition has been said to heal man from this burden. It is the act of becoming more conscious and aware of how you think and how you feel.

The conscious mind can heal us from this cycle of self torture that I mentioned earlier in this chapter, since this mind is the originator of thought, and the act of repeating these conscious thoughts can only result in the rewiring of a new program. New program equals new condition–new conditions equals a new life.

~*THE BODY*~

I am going over the body because it also plays a part in who it is that you are today but it is not you. The body has been said to carry on the identity of who it is that you truly are. This temporary product that we have been blessed with has unique properties of its own. Everything that I described about the subconscious mind ultimately is the body. This body acts as a sponge when being encountered with this 3 dimensional world.

When I went to West Africa around the age of 10, from the United States, I had no idea what I was getting into. I went to a foriegn land because my auntie felt like it was necessary that I'd learn about the culture, dues of my "stubborn ways' ', whatever that means. This experience I had in Africa was an unforgettable one. Being in Nigeria brought out a peculiar side of me. I started to notice my attributes beginning to change such as my accent, my skin complexion, my development of a new language etc. It was interesting to recall how my body began to respond to that environment.

Now remember, the body's natural function is to protect the skeletal system and all the important organs and stuff. Other than protecting the sensitive tissues and nerves, the body also protects us in a unique way. In order for the body to feel safe in its current environment it will try its best to unapologetically scope out its current environment. Now, once the body has successfully done this it will begin to act as part of that environment in order for you to feel safe. The body's slogan is *"if you can't beat them, simply be them"*. I mean you can see this attribute take place in almost anything, like being amongst your friends (show me your friend and I will tell you who you are), being among people who seem to be more confident than you (surround yourself with the people you would like to become). The robot has a tendency to conform. Why do we conform? I mean come on let's face it, we weren't given a blueprint on how we should live these lives unless you were to read the Holy Bible or the Holy Quran but let's say you weren't the type that was brought up in a religious household then what? We more than likely allow ourselves to conform to that which we are surrounded by.

Like I said before, this body is like a pet if you train it properly then it will obey you, but if you have no type of care for this pet then it will disobey you like a stray dog with rabies, literally. Self does have a lot to do with your external bodily features, like the law of correspondence states, "as within so without". Your body reveals who you truly are, take care of it and it will take care of you, you only get one of these things so use it wisely. This kind of reminds me of a woman that was diagnosed with a bipolar and schizophrenic disorder, when I spoke to this woman and asked her what caused her symptoms her simple response was "the changing of the environment."

It occurred to me that she missed her home so much to the point where it caused chronic depression, her soul and heart had been crushed on the inside because she thought she would never get a chance to see her home again and she believed those thoughts, which caused the outward expression of her distressing symptoms.

This body, to my understanding, is a force that acts as the magnetic pull to the things we want as well as that which we don't want. It is the reflection of the inner world. When you know who it is that you are, the body tends to take the form of who it is you are becoming. Your body is one with the soul and based on the things your body has experienced, it can either mold the soul into something that it is not or the body can simply submit to the soul and become what it was designed to be. The body is an amazing communicator as it responds well to the environment and translates it to the brain which shapes one's conditions.

The body is important and I reckon that you shower it with material blessings. Spoil yourself from time to time, eat well, and workout! That is how we attract good things outta life, the good partners, better sex, good friends, better opportunities. The body is literally the reflection of one's soul, you gotta be able to look at yourself in the mirror and be proud of how far you came. This is a spiritual journey in a physical experience. F the critics, F the naysayers, you are in control of this body and how it is supposed to feel at all times!

Never and I repeat never let another robot influence your robot's functions, feelings and or thoughts.

~*THE SOUL*~

I once read something that said that there is more to us than just meat and bones. As odd as that may sound, it is true. I must say that within the depth of this complicated construct of this human body lies an indestructible force known as the soul. This soul in spiritual terms is said to be the light that gives this body its natural glow that others tend to complement us about. The soul is the beginning of all creations as well as the end. This soul is you. It has been said that the soul is the only thing on this body that can connect with infinite intelligence, some like to call this intelligence "the creator" others like to call this "God, Allah" etc without the soul there will be no way for this robot to feel these unique experiences. Our soul operates by two poles and that is either by faith or by fear. What I love about our abilities as precious souls is that we have the power to choose between these forces which can overall impact how our bodies will eventually turn out. Bob Proctor explains how the expression or suppression of the soul can either lead to depression or acceleration. I was watching one of his videos on youtube and he explained how the body responds to the nature of the soul. While watching this video I learnt that lacking knowledge in the things we sometimes want to improve usually is the cause of fear and anxiety throughout the body. This eventually leads to suppression of those feelings, which causes depression, then disease then decay. Our soul can literally be so crushed to the point where it can actually kill this physical body. Whereas on the other side of that coin lies the concept of understanding. The knowledge I was able to learn about the concept of understanding as it relates to the soul literally blew me away. I realized that a soul of understanding is what causes the emotion of faith throughout the body. When you are able to understand a situation to its entirety it leaves you with a sense of ease and comfort, because not only are you aware of the cause of the situation you are also aware of the solution. From the feeling of faith then leads to habit the of well being which is usually express outward as a result from the reflection within, after a piece of you has been able to express itself, this then leads to the acceleration towards one's accomplishments or goals or desires which ultimately rests in a person being at ease with oneself. Then finally the creation. This can be the creation of a new self, a new life, whatever! The concept is observing that overall "understanding leads to creation, but you have to follow those steps first,

What I just explained was basically the evolution or de-evolution of your true self, which is the soul. YOU can make or break YOU. The ability to choose is not done by your mind, it is done by you as a soul. You have been blessed with a robot that has been equipped with some substantial machinery such as the mind, the heart, the limbs etc. and you have been out in the passenger seat to lead the way. It is you that HE selected for your body, (and me), so use your robot to its fullest capacity, stretch your wing and soar, not literally! Figuratively.

CHAPTER TWO

SELF LOVE

What is love to the world if you haven't shown that love to

yourself.

~Onyekachi

Love is the intense affection that one shows to a significant other, family member, friend, and most importantly to one's self. This was one of the emotions that I struggled to develop within myself. I realized that I couldn't accomplish my heart's desires if I couldn't love myself first. As a man I realized that I could not love a woman properly if I hadn't loved myself first. I failed to understand the true meaning of love. I wonder why. I wanted to know the source of why I wasn't able to properly love myself and after the distinct reminiscing I understood that the way I was brought up allowed me to despise myself deeply. I would say it was because I was constantly criticized by my family on every single thing that I had done or would do. Literally everyone if not, 95% of my family somehow developed this preconceived notion that I was going to be some bad child that would end up on the streets somewhere , even worse end up like my mother (yea my moms had it pretty awful) and to prevent this thought that they originated from happening I was scrutinized like a scientist with a microscope. Because I couldn't understand the right concept for love I started opening up my mind and looking at love with a whole new outlook, and my perception of love miraculously changed the formation of my brain wave. I understood that Love is everything. I mean literally, everything. Don't believe me, ok watch this. Love is forgiveness , love is the plants that grow to give us oxygen, love is crazy, love is blind, love is jealous, love can even be hate, love is the sun that rises in the morning, love can be annoying, love can be confusion, love is "oops baby i'm so sorry", love is distant, love is eternal love is literally everything you can think of. I could probably write a whole encyclopedia describing the metaphors of love.

Some may say hate is the opposite of love, well not in this book. In this book love is hate, I mean you can literally love a person to the point where you would want them hurt, dead or in jail. You can literally hate yourself for the amount of love you have for a person. Love is toxic and love is beautiful. In this book there are only two types of love: natural and artificial.

See we as human beings possess both of these. The body loves, and the soul loves too. I explained earlier in this book that the soul makes up the essence of who we are, which is true, but that does not deny the fact that this body has a mind of its own. We are in constant battles with the wants of the body as well as the wants of the soul. The body can love just as much as the soul and we sometimes get this misconstrued.

I honestly don't know what love is, let me rephrase that I don't know what society thinks love should be. Love has been so dumbed down to the point where we have 5 love languages. I mean I get the concept but I realized that the most important love there is the one you have towards yourself. The natural love we have should not be wasted on just anything or anybody. Your love is valuable and precious and should be treated like the rarest thing to exist, "preserved". Now to get a better understanding of love let's be clear that there are only two major types of love, as I stated before, and they are natural love and artificial love. Now I am not saying that one is better than the other (it's natural love) but what I am saying is that in order to properly love oneself these two concepts of love should be understood.

~NATURAL LOVE~

This type of love is real, genuine energy. The bird that chirps and the flowers that bloom is all part of this natural love. The sun that shines and the rain that falls is also part of this natural love. Every living thing in this world has this type of love, even the green fungus that grows in the cracks of a leaking water pipe. But how does this love relate to us? Thank you for asking this question whoever you are. As you may know this natural love is the God given love that has been instilled into every single last one of us at birth.

This is the love that the mother possesses and the love that the father teaches. Natural love is real love and it can only be expressed because it is what we possess (bars). That so-called "toxic" love that you guys might have stumbled into at some point in your lifetime was really natural love, it is due to the lack of experience in understanding each other that definitely made that relationship toxic. Natural love is always replenishable whenever it has been wasted on the wrong things, which means that it can never run out. This love can be transformed into something greater than we can even fathom. This type of love in my opinion is truly the best kind of love there is.

To continue my story from earlier, I grew up not knowing how to express love, I always felt like someone had to love me first before I was able to do so, and sometimes I still feel this way. When I grew up and began to gain some type of sense, I noticed that I didn't really have it like my cousins did. I mean they had loving parents in their life but I grew up without a mom or dad. That schizophrenic woman that I told you guys about in the first chapter was actually my mother, and my dad was living in poverty back in Nigeria. So it was just my aunt, my uncle, my cousins and I. Although gratitude was the most important thing to express during that time, I still always felt like my aunt was a little cruel growing up, I guess it was just another form of love she was expressing which was ``tough love". Growing up in an African household was like boot camp every day. Constant yelling, belt lashes and punishments was what I faced as a kid growing up, at one point I started taking this personally. Despite my tendencies of being so stubborn and hard headed, I still felt like everyone in my family despised me because of the burden my mother put on them. This led to me despising my own self, I felt hurt, traumatized, mentally worn and abused growing up. As if that wasn't bad enough I was sent to Africa at the age of ten where the love I felt there was actually real but I still couldn't register in my mind what I did to deserve being sent to a third world country. I was confused, I felt abandoned, and I honestly felt like I wasn't loved by anyone. Being so young I was just going with the flow of things and I had no choice but to make the best of it.

"American boy touch's down in Africa" was the talk of the town in my city back in Lagos, Nigeria. Even though I was sad because of my cousins and friends that I left back home in the US, the kids in Lagos were fascinated by me, I almost felt like a celebrity. During my time spent in Nigeria, I was bouncing from house to house because my auntie who chose to take care of me while I was there was always traveling to Dubai for some apparent reason. I got a taste of living with about 10 different families anytime she left the country. Yes 10! I was pawned off like a used dirt bike, and gullible ol' me was just taking in everything. It got to a point where my aunt and uncle back in the US weren't even calling to check up on me anymore and at that moment I really thought I would be there for good. Being so naive at the time I really didn't know how to respond to anything at all. Although I would love to explain how a 10 year old American boy survived in Africa, I think I'll just save that for another book.

The inability to replenish your natural love can allow you to do damaging things to your body like irresponsible drinking, heavy smoking, constant negative expression of emotions etc. The soul does its best to give its natural love to the body in order for the body to heal from the damages which it had to experience. But by being in an unloving environment this can cause you to give this love to other things rather than holding it for yourself.

When I came back to the United States I was still doing things that still seemed to get my family mad, when in reality I was finding different ways to really discover myself. Being so caught up in the American lifestyle I began to stay out late with friends and smoke weed not because I was trying to be disrespectful to my family, but because I was finally getting a chance to be myself without people judging me, I was getting a taste of freedom. In an African household everything that I mentioned is a no no. I did everything you shouldn't do in the "things African kids should not do" handbook, including going to jail. My family was tired of me and I was tired of my family at the time, so I did what any broken child would do and left home at the age of 19. I was out in the big world all alone trying to figure it out. It was in those two years that I left home where I realized the most important key to life, and that is **SELF LOVE.** All my years of growing up my attention was diverted to friends, family, work, school and other miscellaneous things and I was forgetting the most important factor which was myself. It was when I diverted my attention to myself that I started realizing how smart I really was, how good looking I was and how well I could actually speak to people. I began to notice my flaws and how I could deal with my flaws in such a judgemental society. I understood what I was good at and what I sucked at, I understood who was deserving of my love and attention, and who wasn't. I came across amazing people that could change lives with words alone, and I came across energy drainers, I was able to experience certain types people that only check up on you either to be nosy and people that check up on you because they actually care, I met fake envious friends and I met genuine friends, I came across people that wanted to see me win in life and people that would rather me fail. I met them all, things I wouldn't have experience living with my family. I understood that the attention you give to yourself is the most important gift you can give you, it allows you to open your eyes and to see your world with clarity. The natural love that your soul gives to the body allows you to become more present and self aware of your surroundings and the people that you allow into your energetic aura. Self love is the highest vibration that any human being can and should vibe on and it is vital to your spiritual evolution and physical growth.

I am a firm believer in the saying "material possession does not make a man or a woman who it is that they are", but I insist, spoil yourself from time to time, eat good food, and exercise. This is the physical way of telling your body "I love you." Love yourself for who it is that you are, and who you are is a soul of limitless potential.

~ARTIFICIAL LOVE~

Just like the name says artificial love is simply the love that is not real. I.e it is love that is fake, a facade, temporary, an inorganic way of expressing love. It is love that passes like the wind never to return again. This is the type of love we really should have under control. This kind of love can lead to any man or woman's fall in life. Examples of artificial love can be the love of money, the love of one's ideal self image based on the projections given by society (ego) , the love of materialistic possessions like clothes , cars and jewelry etc., the love of lust (the most dangerous of them all in my opinion), the love of attention and so on and so forth.

Artificial love can be likened to a self portrait, once you say I love you to this portrait it will say nothing back. Due to the body having a mind of its own, the body likes to think that everything that shines is glitter and gold. The body wants the world and everything that dwells within it. If you give an untrained body some sugar it will scratch the back of your hand and beg for some more. Artificial love is one of the most illogical ways of expressing love in my opinion, this is because this type of love always has an expiration date and tends to eventually crumble. First things first, you can never love a man-made object, this is because it is something that can neither feel nor reciprocate the love that you are giving it, so rationally speaking it is hands down a waste of your precious energy. Ok, so what if it is something that you created would you say that it is wrong to love then? Well to answer that question, that love shouldn't be given to what you created, instead you should give that love to yourself for having the courage to do what others won't do except if you created another life then you want to love that creation to death.

I personally don't believe in showing fake love towards a human being. One may say that they have love for a person but their actions may differ and there are many reasons why this can take place. One of the reasons may be the relationship a person may have towards their significant other, there may be certain qualities that one may dislike about that other person which can cause them to show love in a certain type of way. For example, my aunt who expressed love in a vile way. It may be because this was the only way that she knew how to express love, or maybe because of the way she was taught on how to show love, or even how she received love. This was something that I had to understand, and with the amount of belt lashes I got as a kid growing up I now know that that woman loved me to death. Another example may be "loving people from a distance" . This is a term that I had to apply in my life for various reasons.

Although we may have shared fond memories with each other, things eventually change, life has a way of knocking me upside the head forcing me to "embrace the change already" and the things that I once used to enjoy with you can no longer serve me any more which eventually caused me to part ways.
~Onyekachi.

I'm sure many people like myself try to stay away from people who tend to show "fake love", when in reality, it's not fake love at all. It is either that a person does not know how to truly express love or, because a person may actually despise you for some apparent reason and try to use a smile or a clever comment or two-to cover that feeling up. I used to be the first person I just described. I did not really know how to show love to people not because I didn't want to, but because I didn't know how to, maybe because I never got an opportunity to receive the proper love, which therefore caused me to become a bit introverted with my expression of love. I would always get annoyed when I would lose valuable people that I actually wanted to build a serious connection with. For some reason I kept getting a vibe that I was being weird, I can admit I was a bit socially awkward but I was conscious enough to know what was going on. My advice to you before you try to discard a valuable soul from your perspective is to always **"LOVE FIRST, TEACH SECOND".** You love people first by having a keen sense of judgment towards them, try your best to understand a person fully and thoroughly before making any bold and sudden moves, and teach second by showing these individuals through your actions; those that don't know how to express love, show them love like never before, get to know them a little more, connect with them because these unique individuals could be the answer to a problem that didn't even know you had, and those who envy you, simply avoid them by paying them no mind at all. Trust me you'll be able to tell the difference.

Living in a world where artificial love runs rampant in society can sometimes affect the way we as human beings lean on showing real love, this was something that I was able to consciously observe. I understood that my improper output of love towards myself, things that I owned and towards the wrong people was the cause of me being so tired, drained and exhausted. I was able to overcome this by giving more attention to myself by spending more time with myself and also by being still, it felt like I had just healed myself from the impurities that had been lodged in my veins from all of the self negativity and verbal sabotage I bestowed on myself, who would have known that the cure to all this would have been self love and God of course, Love all because all is love,

but love yourself first so that all can love you.

CHAPTER THREE

SELF TRUST

Self trust is the first secret to success.

~Ralph Waldo Emerson

"It's A, no it's B, you know what, it has to be C, screw it we're going with C". Test results come in, "dang it, I knew it was A"! The act of second guessing your decision is perhaps the most common mistake humans tend to make.

I guess multiple choice examples could probably work best for high school or college students. I on the other hand am actually a college drop out which has me wondering why I even used that example, so here's a better one, if you say you are going to be rich, BELIEVE IT! If you say you are going to become a success story, BELIEVE IT! If you say that you are going to break the Guinness book of world records for the longest bubble gum chewer, BY ALL MEANS, BELIEVE IT! We as human life forces cripple our own possibilities to a more abundant experience life has to offer. The moment we doubt the things that we affirm for ourselves is the moment we have given up all that life has to offer. There is a saying that I heard one of my mindset coaches tell me a while back which goes "if you say you can or can't either way it goes you are right."

Self trust is the act of believing in the things that you tell yourself, which can be very beneficial to us human beings when climbing towards the pinnacle of our desired goal, but self trust can sometimes be a double edged sword depending on the concepts of philosophy we want to make our own.

Earlier in this book I compared human beings to a robot because like a robot, we humans should have a function. As humans we should learn to trust the pieces of information, process of thought or even a hunch of inspiration which we possibly tend to receive throughout the day, which can help us in the achievements of certain tasks that we give ourselves. One must learn to obey these thoughts, because these thoughts may serve as stepping stones towards one's freedom of action and desired results.

For some reason as I got older, I was always considered to be a rebellious child. At the time I never sought to figure out why this was the case, but I know damn sure it wasn't because I chose to drop out of school to chase my dreams, or because I chose to move out of my families house at the age of 19, or because I hardly ever listened to my Nigerian guardians (aunts and uncles). No..., it was because... ahem, ok maybe that was why I was considered to be rebellious. Perhaps I was being rebellious in the perception of others, but in my defense I was exercising something that we all possess and that is the instinct of self trust. According to an article that I read about self trust,

Self trust means constantly staying true to yourself to its core, it means to look after your own safety, needs and well being, self trust is knowing deep down that you can survive difficulties, and refusing to give up on yourself.

Earlier when I was describing why I may have seemed rebellious in my family's eyes, there is an important factor that I would like for you to take into consideration and that is, every decision that I made, "I" chose them. The act of sticking with your decision is perhaps the best form of self trust which can be portrayed by any human being. Now I'm not saying that you are above all people and that their opinion doesn't matter, but what I am saying is that you do have the right to assess what is strictly good for you vs what is not so good for you. Take me for instance, I'd always take the first thought that pops up in my mind seriously, I call my first thought my most confident mind and it usually is the most accurate mind that gets me out of my tough situations. If I were to allow my body to obey it, I'd usually feel good about myself for having the courage to act on it immediately, but that still doesn't mean that it always works out in my favor. I have come to understand that even when the choices that you make in life may not seem to be the right choices in the heat of the battle, it doesn't make them ineffective. There is a law which is known as the law of cause and effect simply states that, *"we reap what it is that we sow"*, which could mean that some bad choices may not be all that bad (hear me out). Look at it this way if you were to make a dumb ass decision, it may

more than likely lead to the feelings of

embarrassment, shame, guilt, disappointment,

self disapproval, awkward timidity and all that

other negative harvest that comes from a dumb

decision sown, but those that chose to rise out of

that temporary fuck up, usually double back and

make a better decision which ultimately results in

an even better harvest which more that likely

wipes out the previous fuck ups that we tend to

make. Do you know why that is? Well I believe, it is

simply because you trusted yourself and made the

effort to bounce back from that dumb decision.

Self trust is self confidence. I truly feel like in

order to know whether you are truly confident

about who it is that you say that you are, then

there must be some type of action that should back that up. One can not merely think in his mind that he is the smartest in the class without being able to prove it through his action. The thought is definitely the first step into proving this to yourself, the actions which then follow these thoughts will prove to the world whether you are who you say you are. It is also important to remember that the actions that follow your thoughts on who it is that you are is not to prove to others, but it is to prove to yourself. The moment you do it for others, is the moment the demons of doubt and fear start to creep into your magnificent aura. I've said this before and I'm gonna say it again, F the critiques, and F the naysayers, even if they are your own family members or friends. If you feel that there is something special about you, then that is the truth, it is only left for no one else but you to believe that shit and own up to it.

All my life I was moving out of fear, anxiety and frustration thinking that I would never be what it was that I said I would be. I would begin to start something like a project or a new idea with a mindset of being the best at it, but for some reason, I would never finish it. I realized and started to understand that I was becoming a people pleaser. I wanted everyone to be impressed by the person that I claimed to be, I guess to hide all of my insecurities or something. I would literally act like something that I am not just to fit in and be liked by everyone. I noticed back when I was in high school the kids who were most liked were always considered the popular students. I wanted popularity. I started becoming a class clown, getting into fights, and getting on people's nerves just for the attention.

As I got to my senior year I noticed my popularity status rose a whole lot compared to when I first attended an American high school. I think it was because of a big fight that I got into with an underclassman almost knocking him out. I mean I was trending all on social media getting ridiculous amounts of views. I dressed up like a nerd because it was senior nerd day, so the headline of the fight was, "dude gets knocked out by a guy in church shoes." Although I liked all the attention I was getting, I still begged my friend who posted the video to take it down because of my fear of getting expelled, or even worse, one of my family members coming across the video. It was tough getting him to agree because that fight brought a lot of traffic to his page, but eventually he understood and finally took it down.

As I got older I started to notice the habit of pleasing people beginning to mature. As I got into college, I was drawn towards the cool people because I wanted to be them. I can honestly say making the decision to drop out of college kind of gave me a better taste and understanding of the real world. Even though I failed crucially at the things I onced pursued, it still gave me a better perspective about life, and that is we can be anything it is we want to be. I understood that being liked by everyone was actually a vice which can hinder one from growing into their fullest potential. Instead of being liked by everyone I chose to be respected. Trying to be liked by everyone got me nowhere but the bottom of the barrel. I wanted to please everyone so much to the point where I would put their needs before my own, causing me to unknowingly lose value in myself. This overall led me to doubt my own capabilities. I wanted respect, I still do till this very day. This meant that I had to put myself first and earn that respect, not in a rude and obnoxious way, but in a way which lets people know that I was brought into this world to take care of my own needs and those that are important to me. It meant that I had to live out my purpose and seek a fuller expression out of life. And the most unfortunate thing about that is some people will actually despise you for that. It is not your job to help them understand why they should like you but it is your job to trust the thing that you say you want to do and accomplish it without being afraid of who's on your side or not. The people who trust themselves will always attract people who they can trust if they really pay attention.

Never let loyalty be the cause of your slavery, never let the guilt of the people you once used to be cool with stop you from discovering you self, avoid the dream killers and the doubters from corrupting your magnificent aura, I repeat even if they are you family members or your own friends. If you are able to show them the vision through your actions, they should still love you no matter what and if they don't that is between them and GOD. To live in your truth means to live in the world that you see for yourself, and that my friend is "SELF TRUST".

On the other side of this chapter, I wanna talk about how self trust can turn out to be a double edge sword. Self trust is self confidence, too little of it; you'll be run over like bowling pins in a bowling alley, too much of it and you can be considered a self centered, narcissistic jerk.

Having too much trust (overconfidence) in yourself can sometimes cause you to rely on yourself a little too much. This may not necessarily be a bad thing at first but it could affect you in the long run. Overconfidence is arrogance, and a lot of people who may seem like they know what it is that they are doing can sometimes possess this trait. I must admit I was one of those people who possessed this stuck up trait.

Back when the whole pandemic thing started I was presented with an opportunity to take part in a multi-level marketing organization. I was actually in love with the whole idea of the profession because there I met successful men of all kinds. Their walk, the authority when they spoke, the confidence in their stance etc. was what I wanted to make my own. As I began my journey in this industry, I began to emulate the successful men in the organization. Before you know it, it felt like I had already made it. People started looking at me and began to notice that I actually had what it takes to be successful in this industry. Although I was very young and considered "fresh meat" to the industry, I never really developed the mindset nor the discipline to actually thrive in a competitive industry like that. Instead I was more focused on my charm and how I presented myself with my fancy jewelry and my sharp business attires. I managed to reel in a couple potential recruits to my team but for some reason I just never developed enough self confidence to earn their stickability. I mean I know that's what comes with the business, people come and they go, but at the time I wasn't looking at it from that point of view. I started thinking that everything aside from me was the problem and for some reason I felt like I could do better on my own. I felt like if I would just part wave from my upline (the person who got me started in the profession) I could surpass him and be a better mentor than him and everybody. I wanted to win in the business. "I mean I have the looks, I have the posture, what could possibly go wrong", I asked myself. I'd have to admit though, I did have some guts considering I was a fresh piece of meat to the industry because I actually meant what I said. Unfortunately it wasn't as easy as I made it seem in my mind. I mean I literally went out into the world thinking that I could build a multimillion dollar organization all by myself. Life humbled me real quick. I ignored everything the company had to offer to help me thrive. I lost friends, potential business partners, even mentors because of my arrogance. I really thought I was better than everyone else because I had the looks of a successful business man which I can now see is a terrible measuring tool for one's success. I had to learn that even if I do want to adopt that kind of mindset today, I would have to understand that the only person I should be competing with, is myself.

When things didn't go how I planned I lost so much confidence in myself, I was depressed and agitated with my results. I realized that in order for me to heal from this, I had to trust myself. I had to learn to trust others first and I also had to learn how to value other people's opinion because I realized that not everyone means you harm. I think I watched or read something a while back that said "*you are what you see in other people.*" I wish I could tell you the source of that message, but I do find that statement to be powerful. I noticed that if

I could trust you, that means that I could trust myself. I still do stand by that concept till this day, but I still have to be deliberate in the people that I want to listen to or trust.

I sometimes listen to my parents because of their wisdom but that doesn't mean that they are always right, so I tend to limit the amount of advice that I take from them and only take what I feel is beneficial to me. I am more likely to seek advice from the people who already have the result that I want, like Charlamagne tha God, or people like Steve Harvey and Aliko Dangote. I knew that if I could trust them based on the stories that they told to earn the success, then more than likely I could believe and trust in myself too. Most importantly, I always listen to myself. I know myself better than anyone else and I know that the "self" that I listen to will always be my higher self guiding me to seek a fuller expression out of life and in the likeness of the most high.

CHAPTER FOUR

SELF DISCIPLINE

"Self discipline is when your conscience tells you to do something and you

don't talk back"

W.K Hope

I intentionally put this chapter right after the chapter of self trust because I feel like these two qualities intertwine with one another. Ok, I'm lying, it was never my intention but I do feel like the sequence of these chapters was definitely destined to be in this exact order.

Self discipline is what gives our actions the power to save us from our misery. Self discipline is literally what molds us into who we were meant to be, without it we would be likened to something without any type of form, frame, or grit kinda like mash potato just mushy and out of shape.

Discipline sucks, it really does, but it helps. The moment you decide to change the course of your life for a better one, discipline is what is needed to propel you. I never had anything go well without self discipline. Like I mentioned before, I was the type of guy to hang out with friends, smoke weed and crack jokes all day, even worse I would talk about life and reminisce like an old head who fought in the vietnam war.

I am currently reading one of Charlamagne tha God's pieces of literature titled "Black privilege" (a really great book by the way), and in this book he explained how he never wanted to end up like the guys that would get drunk under a tree just to talk about life. When he wrote about these people he described them as having no kind of dream nor motivation towards their future. The only thing I could think of while reading that was their lack of goals, and discipline to achieve those goals. I was literally that kind of person that he described. Instead of getting drunk underneath a tree to reminisce about life, I was the type to smoke weed in the car or in abandoned buildings with my buddies to talk about life and other things that I could hardly remember. I would be so caught up in the moment, to the point where I would just let time pass me by. Now for some this may be therapeutic, a lot of people get great ideas from these types of gatherings but the ability to execute on these ideas and to persist on these ideas is what most people don't do, this is what makes discipline so important.

Discipline is a quality that you should consider like a friend who shows nothing but tough love. I can say that I am blessed to be raised in an African household. There is a biblical verse which says in Proverbs 13:24, "He who spares the rod hates his son, but he who loves him disciplines him diligently." For some reason this verse right here definitely rang bells in the cities of Nigeria, simply because discipline and respect were the two key attributes drilled into the heads of the youth back home (Africa). I witnessed teenagers, even young adults being flogged with my own two eyes. For some reason it felt like there was nowhere I could go when I was in Lagos, Nigeria (where I lived at the time) to escape an ass beating. If you did something stupid, the elders had the right to knock some sense into your brain. They sometimes use belts, but most of the time they use this wooden stick called a "cane", to either whack the palm of your hand, on your behind, or even all over your body (they call this one "merciless beating"). Prior to me even going to Nigeria I was already raised up on butt whoopings. You remember my aunt I told you about earlier? Let's just say she was a really strict disciplinarian. There are people who are considered regular disciplinarians like the police force, or your high school football coach, or your personal trainer. Then they are the strict disciplinarians like the army, the navy and the marine corp, oh yea and my aunt. I feel like the only reason why I got sent to Nigeria was because I told one of the teachers that I was getting my ass whooped mercilessly at home. Well this teacher in particular asked. Truly, I was a hard headed kid in elementary school, I played rough and was always getting into serious trouble and then suddenly my counselor realized how many times I was getting suspended from school and she wanted to know how these situations were being handled at home. So she called me to the office one day and asked, "how does your aunt deal with you at home?" I told her the truth, not because it was the right and honest thing to do, but because honestly I thought she would save me.

Every time I would get a phone call home, the feeling of straight terror would fill up in my chest, my palms would begin to sweat, and my heart would begin to pace because I knew I was going home to face "the belt" as soon as I crossed those first steps leading front door.

My aunt was pissed off at the fact that I told the school what usually happens to me when I would get in trouble. So she swore she would never put her hands on me. "Whew, what a relief!" I thought, until I got hit with a plane ticket to Nigeria. At least I got a chance to experience the luxury of an international plane flight.

I think sending me to Nigeria was her best option at the time, probably to avoid any of the issues with the US child services. I really don't know her reasons, but I do know that when I got to Nigeria I couldn't call the police or tell my teachers that my elders at home were whooping me so much. In that land if you were a youth, and called the police to report that you were being whipped, the police would pull up to that house, add to that whooping. They would say you are bold for even thinking we would come and help you.

I would get whooped in school by the teachers (yes, the teachers) for failing a test, or for coming to school late, or for making too much noise in class when the teachers weren't there, even for not even ironing my uniform for school. I was whooped so many times that my skin grew another skin to protect my real skin. I learnt that in order to avoid this cruel and unusual punishment, I would have to undergo a serious change in character and demeanor. I realized that when I showed characteristics of a level headed, responsible young man (i.e discipline and respect), I wouldn't get whooped as much. So I took those traits and ran with it. Yea I was still getting smacked around from time to time but the main idea that I realized was I just had to play their game to win, and the key to that game was DISCIPLINE.

When I returned to the US, I realized how different I was compared to the rest of the kids my age. I could literally see the difference in my work ethic, my tolerance towards stressful situations, my sharp intellect from constant studying back in Nigeria (FYI, there wasn't anything like an easy access to google or siri back home, books were our go-to source of information when preparing for exams). I was so confident in the little things that I could do because I had developed so much discipline. It got to a point where I started thinking I was some type of superhero or golden child that had the ability to do things in a way others would actually like to see things get done.

Discipline was what I needed to survive my butt whooping phases. Even though I was living in fear from "the cane", I was still building my character through discipline without even realizing it.

Now I am not saying that you need to get your ass beat to develop discipline (some of you probably do), but I got to realize that we live in a world filled with body builders, successful entrepreneurs, musicians, and artists all striving to be the best versions of themselves they could possibly be, it would be nearly insane to say that one can master themselves and succeed in this kind of eco chamber without discipline. It's like trying to make a car drive on square wheels. Too corny? Ok, let me think of a better example. It's like trying to drive a car with no engine, "oy vey". I'm sure you get the point. Discipline is by far the most important key quality to understanding self aside from self trust. Everyone striving to be better needs it. Success is inevitable with it.

Butt whoopings weren't the only thing that helped me achieve the little things that I never knew I could accomplish like a strong character, resilience and work ethic. It's safe to say that as I got older there wasn't really much my family could do except give me some hefty advice. I realized that at some point in time they weren't going to be there my whole life to correct me if I've done something unfavorable. At some point I was going to have to grow up and do things on my own. Along my journey towards self discovery, I understood that true discipline is not what is done when people are looking but what is done behind closed doors. I had to govern myself and do things I didn't really want to do because that is really what gets you there (to the goal you set out for yourself). I began forming little routines like taking ice cold showers early in the morning, going to the gym often, reading more books etc. I don't know why I enjoy the process the least, but I knew through consistent action I was going to enjoy the results. I realized that not a lot of people take cold showers, that fact alone was what made me start to take 'em. I wanted to separate myself from the pack. Aside from that I noticed a lot of healthier benefits from it, like a more energetic and positive day, my skin looking more radiant, and my thoughts beginning to clear up. When I would take cold showers at night I had a more well rested sleep. I also began to notice a change in my daily methods of operation. Days where I would take cold showers, I would develop discipline in other areas of the day, like making more book sales or connecting with more people, or even picking up a book to read to stimulate my intellect. Whereas days where I would take warm showers because of my inability to endure the cold temperature, I would begin to develop a lazy or even worse a slightly more comfortable day, not all the time, but most of the time. I still take cold showers till this day because I actually feel like it helps, and it is an amazing way to begin the habit of self discipline. Little discipline always results in bigger disciplines being created. Focus on the little things like cleaning your room, or cleaning your car if you have one. Begin a workout routine and stick with it, and most importantly take a cold shower! It helps, it really does.

CHAPTER FIVE

SELF COURAGE

I have not ceased being fearful, but I have ceased to let fear control me

~Erica Jong

What's stopping you? Like really, what's holding you back. You have walked the face of this earth for God knows how long, you've had epiphanies, sudden hunches, deja vu's. You've seen visions of divine and prosperous chapters to come, you've felt rushes of inspiration, you've had dreams while you were awake and while you were asleep of you finally being that person you have always known yourself to be. You have seen yourself actually making it to the place you have always hoped for and prayed for in your mind's eye, so what's stopping you? It's ok to admit it. I am here for you, I understand that it's really tough out here. It's like the moment you actually start to pursue the visions in your mind's eye, forces around you make it hard for you to see. Even when you are aware of these forces it's like you want to make a change but you feel complacent, stuck, and pathetic. Sometimes it may feel like you're running on a hamster wheel or something. You try to fight back but you're like "what's the point or, maybe I'll just wait till things get better". Little do you know the more time you spend waiting, the quicker you die. Suddenly all your dreams you've once cherished begin to fade away and then you become content with the lifestyle that the world around you has handed you. You choose to be contemptuous because you chose to be familiar with the lifestyle of the people who conform to those who conform. Although you are broken on the inside, you don't want to admit it so you hide the shame of not achieving what you knew deep down you could have had at one point in time, with a smile or with a fake expression of laughter. You then slowly begin to develop habits of anger, rage and resentment, pity, hate and bitterness. You get mad at the world when in actuality you forget to be mad at yourself for allowing the death of your desires to erode. Your heart begins to weaken and that glow that you once had has now turned to a dull, worn out, immature victim face or even worse a hateful bitter piece of miserable "bleep".

Sorry for being so blunt but this is honestly what you need. This is what is called the "death phase", the ability of not having the courage to be you. I call this the death phase because you can be alive and still be dead. The good thing about this kind of death is that you can choose to make this death temporary or to last forever, and number two you gain a lot of wisdom and insight once resurrected.

There is a phrase that goes "a valiant man dies but once, a coward lives to die a thousand deaths. Being able to rise out of the death phase requires a lot of courage. Fear is always the cause of any death phase that we may encounter. This world is a scary place, it really is. Other than our close friends and relatives everybody else might as well be considered a stranger. What is even scarier is you don't really know your friends and family the way you think you do, at least not better than they know themselves, so in actuality, all you really got is yourself. You know your fears and that's where the battle line is drawn, you are in constant battle with a part of you that is usually scared to make an attempt, scared to take that leap and the ability to conquer those fears requires courage. There is this author named Ryan Holiday, who made a post on instagram about courage. He mentioned that wisdom is what gives us the insight on what to be courageous about, he outlined the importance of courage, it being the first virtue of the stoics, he said "being courageous is literally making the right choices in life". You can not make the right choices without courage. Courage is the foundation of all of the virtues needed to excel. I find it crazy how it's even hard for people to be their own selves. We've got to break out of that cycle of giving a fuck. You want to build a successful business, but you are worried about what people would think about or what would happen if things were to go wrong, you want to make music but your worried about what people would say about your sound, you want to have the woman (or man) of your dreams but you don't have it in you to be the better version of yourself to attract your desired partner. Shit! If I could cuss in this book then you would probably feel my frustration. Everything I am describing was me at one point. I let the woman of my dreams slip away because I didn't build up enough courage to become a man already. I missed out on millions of dollars because I was too scared to meet new people and build genuine relationships. I was too scared of being myself because I felt like "myself" wasn't worth being shown to the world. I deprived myself of the things that I could achieve because I was a little....

Having the courage to admit your fears and your fuck ups is one of the first steps to developing a courageous lifestyle. But before that you need to understand the cause of your fears and the type of fears they are. For some it could be the fear of missing out (FOMO). This type of fear usually results in lacking the courage to let go of something, or lacking the courage of being alone. Another example of fear could be the fear of failure. This is what most people tend to develop due to the critics always having things to say which usually ends up to one not trying at all. There is a yoruba adage which says, "if you do good or bad in this world people will still have something to say". So if this is true, then there is no reason not to at least try, they're going to talk regardless of what you do. The fear of success is one that is crippling and subtle, some don't even notice they have this fear causing them not to go all out. This was a fear that I once had. I was too afraid of what others would think or do if I had finally accomplished my desires. Obviously I would have had to mature into a more evolved self being more aware of things, which would allow me to do things differently, but would my friends and family understand this? I was too scared to lose people if it came down to that, so I reduced the output of my expression to the world. I limited my own potential because of others i.e. I put others before me.

Being able to go against the norms of society and that of the family to attract the desires which lie within the preview of life's coming attractions in one's own perception of the world -catches air-, is probably one of the greatest acts of courage that one can show. Sometimes, it may be kind of challenging to reach a desired destination due to different people wanting to sway your attention. Living in any type of society can be tough for the weak, it can cause these individuals to end up confused and directionless which causes them to begin to figure out different ways to understand their own function, or what role they play in society. Having to deal with these 'stereotypical preconceived notions' about how one should act in the society, from people who live in the same society is by far one of the most crippling concepts any human species can adopt. If there aren't people "higher in authority", like your parents, or the priest telling you how you should act or behave, then more than likely you are conforming to your peers.. The ability to restrain yourself from being compliant to the thoughts and opinions of you from the perceptions of others, is the act of staying true to oneself, and also the act of showing great self courage.

Certain people don't like it when you are able to authentically be yourself. They despise that trait. This may be out of the fear that you will surpass them or out of the fear that you will amount to nothing embodying such a pompous character , ouch, didn't mean to drop the bomb like that but thats what it is. These people who have their perception over you will most likely be your family and friends. The important thing is to understand that their perceptions can not define you. Their opinions don't even matter. You know who you are because you are who you are. You see this person everyday, you sleep with this person, you imagine what life would be like when this person achieves his or her worthy ideals. So this means that you know who you are, what you stand for and what it is that you want, the only thing standing in the way of that, are your fears and insecurities. The moment you look past those fears and realize that you're all that exist, the floodgates of abundance will be open onto you.

One of my first acts of courage was when I wrote my first book. This gave me the title of being a published author in society. Like I mentioned earlier, I gained a lot of respect from people and I was presented with a lot of opportunities. Being able to perform a courageous act like that gave me poise and confidence in my stance and in the way that I spoke. I understood if I had never written a piece of literature, what would I have been known for? What identity would I have given this body? Yes, I am a soul that lies in this robot, but the expression of this soul is what makes life so beautiful. Having the courage to express who you really are is where the meaning lies, lack of expression is literally equivalent to death.

You must learn to be able to walk freely when you pass through a crowd without worrying about how people are judging the way that YOU walk, be able to pass a stranger in the hallway without quickly pulling out your phone to avoid what they will think about your face, be able to talk with you soul and not with the insecurities imbedded inside your body. At the end of the day it's not what people think about you it is what you think about YOU. Sometimes you might have to separate yourself from the ones that view you as less powerful for you to see the true power you possess. You might have to take a break from certain groups you one took part in for you to see where you really need to develop courage. You need to lead yourself first, study yourself thoroughly. Pay attention to the weakness you possess and seek out ways to develop this, communicate with people that know how to communicate, people who you can grow with. These are all courageous acts. Any movement towards the right direction is courageous. Embody it, breathe it, live it, be it.

CHAPTER SIX

SELF-MOTIVATION

Just do it.

Nike,

I realized that no matter how bad you want something out of life, you can never get it by just laying down watching movies or binge watching shows all day. I am guilty of this. This body is the store house of divine power and abundance, and sometimes we allow ourselves to be dulled out by the limitations of the body.

I always tried figuring out different methods that I could use to keep myself motivated. Sometimes I'd feel as if there is nothing in the world to be motivated by. I remember one time I used to be amped up to play soccer for my high school team. "The Martin Luther King Lions". Although we never brought a trophy home, I was still excited to step out on that field. It was something about the way the lights lit up the field in the night time, and the way the crowd would cheer anytime we or the other team would score a goal, and I wanted to be in that. I understood that if I wanted to end up on that field rather than being on the bench, I would need to condition my body and my mind to be prepared for the upcoming season.

Luckily for us (the men's soccer team) we were fortunate enough to have a big enough field for all the school's sport teams to practice on. They set up an after school training for my soccer team and we were ready to roll.

It was something about our soccer practice in particular that really made me want to quit the whole sport in general. I mean the constant drills, constant laps around the track, the exhausting suicides. I know some of you are probably wondering, "dude, isn't that what comes with the sports?" ok maybe you're not thinking that or maybe you are I don't freaking know! All I know is that I wasn't that "lazy guy" that complained about the work or training that was meant to help anyway, It was just this coach in particular that made soccer a traumatizing experience. I can still hear my coach's voice with his heavy Caribbean accent yelling at us saying, "GO, GO, GO" or something like "PASS THE FREAKIN" BALL, YOU SEE ONE MAN OPEN WHY YOU NO PASS THE BALL!!". Half of the time I wouldn't even hear what the hell he was saying because of the mixture of his aggression and his heavy accent. I had nightmares about that voice. I always thought that man was annoying because he would act as if he hated us. There were so many times I wanted to quit because I couldn't stand his tone of voice and the way he made us do drills that more than likely he couldn't do, but I knew he was only preparing us for our big seasons to come. Something also that I realized was that no one ever pointed a gun to my head saying, "YOU MUST COME TO PRACTICE, OR IT'S OFF WITH YOUR HEAD"! No no no, I really wanted to play ball, I even harassed my uncles for the money to even be a part of the team. "Now why would I do that?" Some may ask. Well, for starters I loved the game of soccer, most importantly I loved the recognition that I would get anytime I were to score a goal and hear my name on the intercom in school the next morning. I also loved the road trips that we would have going to our rivals' territory, I loved cracking jokes with the team anytime we were to lose badly or if someone missed an open shot at the goal, and many more experiences I can't think of right now. And honestly that's really what kept me going every time I wanted to quit during practice. I had no choice but to motivate myself and keep myself moving towards the target if I really wanted those fun experiences that I desired at the time.

Now what is self motivation? Where does it come from? How can one develop this trait? Why is it so important? Well self motivation to my understanding, is an inner work of developing power and strength which pushes the body to create, achieve and repeat. Without the use of this inner work of power and strength, we might just be compared to a log which lies on the ground all day collecting molds and worms and gunk. I don't expect you to take that metaphor literally lol, but I do want you to understand the similarities of a log vs. a person with no self motivation, and that similarity is that neither one has the ability to grow.

Self motivation, I believe, is the component needed to help one to grow towards an ideal self. It helps one finish important tasks and achieve complicated goals. Self motivation is what is needed when no one else is around to give you that push.

Time after Time I'd realize there's not too many people in this world who are really going to push you to where you want to go. This may be because they are looking for the same motivation, the same push, that drive. Most people don't have the motivation which therefore causes them to stay content, complacent and satisfied with what they already have ie. they settle. Usually this is due to them feeling as if there is nothing more out there to accomplish.

Now I can't speak for other people but I can speak for myself. I used to think that there was nothing more for me to achieve, I used to think I was average until I understood that there was a part of me that was never discovered. I know that I'm not perfect, hell nobody's perfect, but that does not mean we should settle for less. There is a soul that each and everyone of us possess which is yearning for so much more expression and we need to utilize this soul to push our body to strive for more.

My body is a reflection of the things that I've experienced in the past and some of those things are not so good, some of those things are de-motivating, and not so encouraging. I've had family members telling me to give up on my dreams and in what I believe in, I've had friends switchgear towards different paths because they didn't really believe in the path we all were walking down at one point, I even had strangers trying to size me up to see if I am who I really say I am. They would judge me because they never could see what I could see. I felt belittled everytime I would experience this but I would always remember this quote from the great Mr. Les Brown where he says "If you judge me now, then you judge me prematurely", that simply means that, just because you're not where you want to be yet, doesn't mean that you're not going to get there. There are countless trials and errors that you have to experience for you to reach a fuller expression of yourself, there are a lot of things that your body has to experience for your soul to be able to magnify the way it wants to.

Self motivation is the only motivation we should really consider, because I believe motivation from any other person may help but it only serves as temporary motivation. You need to be able to push yourself under any circumstance. The ability to create, thrive and grow is solely dependent on how far you are willing to push yourself. Don't ever give up on yourself, and don't ever quit on yourself. **THAT IS AN ORDER.** Your soul is all you have, your soul is your true self seeking expression. Never let the limitations of your body be the cause of you not discovering who you truly are. I said it once and I'm going to say it again: you have limitless potential. Yeah yeah yeah, you might grow old one day and not have the energy that you used to have but the audience that I'm speaking to right now I believe you have what it takes, you have that potential right now! I believe the only limitations are the ones that you set up inside of your mind. It's crazy, I'm literally trying to motivate you the best way that I can because I know self-motivation is really self-explanatory but I do want to use this chapter to reach out to those that don't really feel as if they have so much motivation in their lives.

Go out and chase your dreams, because your dreams lie in the essence that is not seen, which is your soul. Your soul holds the treasures of an unforeseen miracle. The more you are able to push your body, the more you will be able to witness these treasures. You don't need people to tell you what you can and can not do, that's literally what you're for. When you start, make sure you finish. When you fall, you get your ass back up. When they say you can't, show them that you can. Say no to excuses, and push yourself no matter what! I mean it!